Hold and Release

Poetry Books by CB Follett

The Latitudes of Their Going (1993)
Gathering the Mountains (1995)
Visible Bones (1998)
At the Turning of the Light (2001)
Hold and Release (2007)

Hold and Release

Poems by

CB Follett

TIME BEING BOOKS
POETRY IN SIGHT AND SOUND

An imprint of Time Being Press
St. Louis, Missouri

Time Being Books®
10411 Clayton Road
St. Louis, Missouri 63131

Time Being Books® is an imprint of Time Being Press®, St. Louis, Missouri.

Time Being Press® is a 501(c)(3) not-for-profit corporation.

Time Being Books® volumes are printed on acid-free paper.

ISBN 978-1-56809-111-2 (paperback)

Library of Congress Cataloging-in-Publication Data:

Follett, C. B.
    Hold and release : poems / by CB Follett — 1st ed.
      p. cm.
    ISBN 978-1-56809-111-2 (pbk. : acid-free paper)
     I. Title.
   PS3556.O394H65 2007
   811'.54—dc22

                                               2006100760

Cover design by Jeff Hirsch
Cover photo copyrighted by CB Follett
Book design and typesetting by Sheri Vandermolen

Manufactured in the United States of America

First Edition, first printing (2007)

Acknowledgments

The following poems have appeared, sometimes in different versions, in various publications: "Annie's Room" (*Web Del Sol*); "Close Encounter" (*Green Fuse*); "Coming Home" (*Sistersong*); "Considering Endless Nights" (*Heliotrope*); "The Cow, the Moon, a Glass of Milk" (*Pennine Platform*); "Fulcrum" (*RUNES: A Review of Poetry*); "Ice" (*Home Planet News*); "Leather Boys" (*Ploughshares*); "Making the Cut" (*Afterthoughts*); "Mary Isabel Sits in Her Room Looking Down on the Streets" (*Sweet Annie & Sweet Pea Review*); "Not One of Those Girls" (*Poets On: Complaints* and *Poets On: Twenty Year Anniversary Reprise*); "On the Movement of Petals and Feathers" (*Sarasota Review*); "Red Flash" (*Matchbook*); "The Sap of Spring" (*RUNES: A Review of Poetry*); "Stones of Memory" (*RUNES: A Review of Poetry*); "Sunstones" (*RUNES: A Review of Poetry*); "That Red Girl" (*The MacGuffin*); "Time Runs Past but Never Out of Sight" (*The Jabberwock Review*); "Would She Have" (*Sow's Ear Poetry Review*).

"Not One of Those Girls" appeared in *An Intricate Weave* (Iris Editions, 1997).

"Hidden Up" appeared in *Tree Stories: A Collection of Extraordinary Encounters* (Sunshine Press, 2002).

"Coming Home" appeared in *At Grandmother's Table* (Fairview Press, 2004).

"Considering Endless Nights" and "Deep in the Roots" appeared in the *Marin Poetry Center Anthology, Volume VII* (2004).

"Borealis" and "The Cow, the Moon, a Glass of Milk" appeared in the *Marin Poetry Center Anthology, Volume Eight* (2005).

"Another Birthday," "It Happens with Children, Often, Those Things That Scare Us," and "The Swallow" appeared in *Runaway Girl* (Pudding House Press, 2007).

"Hold and Release" appeared in *Hymns to the Outrageous* (Pudding House Press, 2007).

For Lee,
who keeps me safe and lets me run free,
with love and thanks.

With thanks to Susan Terris, David St. John,
my family near and far,
the Stray Poets, the Cloud View Poets,
and all the rest of you
who have been in my corner for so long.

Contents

Hold and Release

backlight

In deference to my family, please keep in mind that the "I" of the poem is not necessarily the "I" of the poet.

(*) This symbol is used to indicate that a stanza has been divided because of pagination.

Fulcrum

Suppose you had not turned your head
when the man with a fiery beard tripped over the curbstone,
whose bed would now be yours,
what complication of molecules, your children.

Red light changes to green,
the moon shuffles behind a squall cloud,
what kind of story waits at the crosswalk to take your hand
and guide you with the flow or against it.

A woman stands by a fountain throwing her lunch to pigeons.
If she brushes off her hands, exits through the south gate
as you swing though the eastern one with your full bag of lunch
        and contentment,
was a vital connection missed or escaped?

My friend, visiting the caves in India
was set upon by a monkey and bitten to the bones of her cheek.
Was it only because a man paused to let her enter first,
and which way would her path have led
without the jagged scar that never smoothed
like an over-wintered apple in the root cellar.

A friend walked the lake path at Treetops,
trailed by ten feet a Dutch woman with bushy hair,
when a water buffalo charged from his soak and killed
before she could open her mouth to scream.
Still holding his second cup of coffee
the man too horrified to move toward or away —
the buffalo turned, and returned, to the water swaying with reeds.

Borealis

From the blue shadows of sleep
I travel over the landscapes of the dead,
riding the currents of years
without guide or rein.

How peaceful — an autumn leaf
tossed from some branch of sky,
I am a plaything of the wind.
Without me, on this night frosted with stars,
who would know the wind had awakened.

Below are occasional galaxies of towns
burning their candle powers,
sucking it up like greedy children.

The sun, in a temper of late, spews
gouts of flame and sear. I look
to the north, sunflares are the promise
of borealis.

But alas, no scrim of wavering light,
such as those we used to see
going home from college dates — late
to check-in because we'd been kissing
on a side street — and suddenly:
magic in the sky. We had to stop.

And the time we flew over the pole
through a night filled with ethereal lights,
over Greenland: the eerie ice below,
the eerie light above, and a full moon,
solid and dependable pulling us forward.

Backlight

Where the sun licks at waves
with its last light;
where dusk pelicans glide for the dunes
on the back side of the spit,
look,
isn't that him?

I stop well away
and watch my heart bucket across the sand
like a loosed kite.
Reckless spirit.
Foolish heart.

I am indecision.
Even knowing what I know
all the ropes of my body strain forward
every muscle, eyes and tongue,
the soft curve of my breasts and belly
the yearning arrow of the groin.

Only my hands work against this pull,
hands and the mind whose corners
remember the past.

A seagull screes and drops near a bread crust,
pecks a firm grip,
takes it a safe distance.

And I haul in the headlong legs,
draw back the arms,
the sweet and sour of other days,
return the brine of love
into dune grass,
into shadow and bracken.

Breaking Winter's Hold

And yet, it's hard to remember winter
after a sun-sated day like today.
Finally the top down on the car — windows down —
sun beating on my shoulders and head,
left arm jaunty on the sill.
It's hard to remember last week
when we were whining about winter —
extra sweaters and retreating light —
but the sun is coming back —
and the dusk lasts later now —
the darkness falls later —
and the stars tonight are crisp and wild —
and the crescent moon holds the full moon in her arms —
I love it when that happens —
and the Horsehead Nebula is a soup of infant stars
and the Crab Nebula is the death ring of an old star
and the plum has flowered and faded in our patio,
its magenta leaves overtaking, and the cherry and apple
wait to bud — and it's time for mushrooms under the camellias,
and out of their winter's rest, daffodils shove upward.

The Sap of Spring

with a bow to Gerald Stern

He lit the buds just forming on the branch-tips,
lit them like candles. The sap of spring
sizzled at the kiss of the match, sputtering,
a tree of buds that would not be candles, as if
his birthday wasn't enough, as if the sky —
nice rich blue — was a blowing wind
that snuffed candles for a living — nice tree,

its bark a ruffled pelt, skin outside skin,
like the summer tan that sloughs off in long
mica-ed sheets. We used to sit at the end
of the dock and peel the boys —
long, curling patches of them —
want to keep them in scrapbooks, but they
were only the stuff of boys who smelled of salt
and hidden cigarettes.

We left their backs tattered like the pinto ponies
we rode on Wednesdays, aiming them
toward the low white fences, hoping
when they jumped they would use
their own good sense and not rely on
messages from our legs — nice ponies

with their mud-caked hoofs
we patent-leather-shined for gymkhanas,
reins loose on their necks, our nice
taut rumps tucked into English saddles,
rounding on the canter — nice leather smell,
rising like tree-sap under us — leather
and some primal woman-smell beginning,

nice smell, the boys thought
sneaking a sniff of saddles in the tack room
the way they used to smell our bicycle seats,
some aphrodisiac they would grow into,
boys with hot eyes that wanted things,
that talked about the things they wanted,
with a can of Schlitz and a Camel, things
they wanted but didn't yet know how to get —
the promise of nice things,

and the ponies, turned out to graze, nibbled
with their fat square teeth,
their nice muzzles soft against the hand
offering carrot, sugar cube,
their brown eyes half-lidded,
right legs cocked — shapely legs —
better than Nancy Betrow's, whose legs
could do things to boys — nice boys
but vulnerable as wheat before the reaper.

The little ponies with their yellow/green teeth,
and their whisk-tails chasing off flies,
brushed our faces, necks, shoulders,
teeth nuzzling, tails whispering —
nice tails — nice ponies.

The Tang of Memory

I remember once feeling that nothing could change,
though in retrospect, I am always
waiting for your approaching shape.
It is time, it has always been time.
You could lift the scrim from this scene
and let sound and the short trill of pipers
crease the shadowed side of what makes us cry.
Salt has a tang that brings memory
and the language of our ears is as one with oceans.
No matter the cost of changing, my heart moves forward.
I wish I could land beached on some shore warm with sun
as the green light of late afternoon whispers for dusk.
No matter how the wind slides through the sightlines of trees
the memory listens only to itself.

Not One of Those Girls

I'm not one of those girls you'd call Babe
or dare to lay on your sweet talk,

not one of those girls who thinks the word
lady connotes anything I ever wanted to be,
who thinks cucumber sandwiches with their
crusts cut off are part of the basic food groups
and I'm not one to let him get away with talking
about the *men* and *girls* at his office,

and yet, girl is what I am after all
with my feet bare and clothes not quite matching, girl
with a good pocket in my fielder's mitt, girl
of trees and ice castles, of an inside curve
and still the girl who wore her first strapless gown
like an erector set with the little bolts missing
from strategic connections.

I'm not one of those girls who *lunch*, and bid *game*
while discussing recipes, not one who settles for the
doctor's, *There, there, dear, don't you worry about it*,
but I'm still a girl who's about thirty years younger than
I've aged to, who carries the eight-year-old and sixteen-
and thirty-year-old as friends of the heart,

and I'm one of those girls whose bones creak,
who begins to acknowledge the fine hand of time
that jerks the body around to remind us
no matter how much we remain one of those girls,
parts of us need more oil than they used to.

I was not one of those girls who listened
to her mother, but snuck out and walked
in the cool breeze of midnight along roads ending
in country, wind stirring the scent of newly opened maple,

and I'm still the girl who got scared of distance
and shadow but kept walking,
and when I got home, I was the girl
who listened to the wringing of my mother's hands
and knew I would go again.

snapshots

Would She Have

If she'd known
would she have let her heart
bleed
toward his would she
have put her safe girlhood
on a shelf in the house
where her parents were graying
under late afternoon clouds
Would she have put out her hand
toward his and said yes if she'd known
how short seven years
how swiftly how impossibly unprepared
If she had known about money
hard to acquire little to be paid
If she had known about the way
his life was ticking down
how even as they married he was
withdrawing closer to the edge
each day taking her closer to the dark
If she had known would she have
the baby would she have
continued to want would they have
worked at having   Would he
have reached out his arms would she
have lain with him would the baby
If she had known would she ever
have met him touched his light hair
followed his steps town to town
would she have asked
about children
would she have left home If she
had imagined the monster
eating from within would she
the baby if she had known the baby
But he didn't she know
they didn't know couldn't see
the hidden the baby would they have
if they'd known   You cannot see beyond
the dark she couldn't see
*

the great dark empty hole
of the heart the baby coming
the going the door ajar
and then closing the light
leaking out the dark
seeping in his hair light
as the stroke of the sun
slipping through the door the door
closing the baby the iron weight.

Coming Home

Two widows, one weathered, one raw.
My mother coming home lost and adrift.
My grandmother settled
into each seam of her house.

Into this house and her welcome, we came,
infant crying and wounded daughter/mother.
And my grandmother willing.

If I disturbed her, she never said.
If she wished the return of old peace,
she didn't show it. Sometimes
when I raced through the house
chased by my yappy terrier, I would hear her
groan from the next room.

We lived over twenty years while her hair
turned from dark to gray to a white so pure
it was blinding. She put up with sleepovers,
long telephone calls, white rats that escaped
and climbed her bedroom curtain.

I tried on whaleboned corsets
with their unbelievable waists,
stone martens that snapped at each other
with stiff, hinged mouths, her wedding dress
kept in the tissue of her past.

We played gin rummy, later canasta.
and when she was old
I'd meld the wrong cards so *she* could win.

The Cow, the Moon, a Glass of Milk

When the cow jumped over the moon,
I looked up at my grandmother. *Cows can't
jump like that*, I said, *can they, Grammy?*

Only this cow, she said turning the page. But later,
outside, the grass damp and deep on my feet
I stared at the moon fattening each night
on the milk of stars. I watched
for the shadow of the cow.

There would be no dish or spoon. I knew
better than that, but a cow might need
to reach the milk-filled moon, like the station
where we got gas, tearing off our ration stamps.
Did the cow, I wondered, need stamps
to fill her udder from the moon tanks?

I always asked for that rhyme at bedtime.
We might go on to the jerky boy who jumped
over flaming candlesticks, or Jack,
who played with his food, silly
and so like boys, but the cow

held possibilities, as she gracefully levitated
over the peaked roof of my house, above
the sleeping village, and set sail for the moon
rising through the chestnut branches.

If she jumped now, straight up, she might
intercept the moon by midnight, and leap
down again to her clover-sweet meadow
before the stir of sun.

My grandmother, not much given
to flights of fancy, willingly poured
a glass of milk that frothed at the lip,
extracted slowly and tantalizingly,
a cookie or two from the jar
kept out of my reach. I would sit

on her warm lap in her warm kitchen,
knowing where the milk came from,
look out at the moon and nod to myself.

Mary Isabel Sits in Her Room Looking Down on the Streets

In this small room of my life, I am too old
to go out into the familiar street below.
I sit here like suet, thick,
holding myself together.

I no longer look in the mirror.
No one I know is there.

Where is the handsome woman
with fourteen-inch waist few could emulate?
Granddaughters rooting in the attic, brought down
my old corset, the stays, lace still at bodice and thigh.
They wanted to know what it was;
even with their pencil-thin youth, their bones
are too big to fasten it.

"You, Grammy?" they chime.
Yes, me. Once. Young men
with stiff collars came to call. We sat trim
as sailboats close to the wind, in my mother's
parlor, she near enough to set
teacups jumping with her eyes.

When I picked Henry, she was surprised.
He's full of air, she said, transparent
as cellophane. Won't stand up well.

But he was kind, of good stock,
and he had ambitions,
fragile as butterfly wings but I believed
in him, put my hand in his

and we moved here, when this street
was lined with elms — a bower —
no cars backfiring. Mostly hooves
and leather creaking. Weekends
were slowful days of visiting. Children
were born up and down the street. First,
our Francis, only a blink from birth
to him dying like that on the capitol steps,
out in the open under the dome
and all the painful life in between.

How Henry died before Helen married
and then Edward, dried out
like a stick by that bohemian woman
he fell in love with, each the worst possible
for the other, but of course, we blamed her.

Before the electric light, I lived,
to after the atomic bomb and each
as big a bang as the other. My dancing parties
were lit by gaslight, flattering,
and no bridges crossed the rivers. We took

raft ferries, all jostled together and the ferryman
pulled us across by overhead rope.
I wished he would let go and we could float
down to the mouth, to the widening harbor
with no Statue of Liberty, though we once
rode the train to the city to see her torch
in Washington Square.

To the Man in the Photograph
on My Mother's Wall

You are the slimmest, not the shortest,
half shadowed in a group of merchants
posed on a sidewalk at the end of town.
You seem as if the meat of life had been rolled
out of you in Grandmother's wringer, the one
in the basement of your house where I grew up,
the wringer I was afraid would grab
my sleeve and suck me into a ribbon like you,

   "Grandfather"

     a word I've never used.

The sepia man with his sepia clothes.
Twenty two years I lived in your house
where you raised your family, fought
against spiders. I never heard Grammy
mention your name, your place in her heart.

I would like to hear from you.

Were there no greens and blues, no reds?
What did you think of when your women
crisped their mouths like the starched
and ironed folds of linen napkins.
Your daughter does not like to talk about you.

She could not forgive you for the grayness
you tracked into the house. Animal prints
you didn't know you were leaving,
she hunted relentlessly as drops of blood.

Did you have birthmarks? Did you bite your nails?
What objects collected lint in your pockets
and what of her blue hat
with half a bird slapped on one side — the one
in your honeymoon picture?
Were you sexy as a fox?

You look as if all the green growing
had dried out of you, as if I could snap you
in two like a twig from the brush pile.
Your house gave no smell of you being there.

I imagine families gathered on streets
without cars, women sailing the roadbed
like galleons and men in white linen suits,
straw hats set straight on their heads
but I can't see you.

5" x 7" — you exist there on the wall
or in a half-dozen darkened snapshots
stuck into albums,
some of the little gummed Vs gone.

Ice

From the Rockies to Atlantic hatcheries,
ice sheaths the land.
Rivers slow to a thick stop. The old
are house bound, snow banks swallow cars,
even dogs keep their cut pads in shelter.

I call my mother.
It's an ice palace, she says,
Never storms like this in my lifetime.
I remind her about driving cars
on Long Island Sound. *Before my time;*
you should have asked your grandmother.

•

In Chicago, an old woman living alone
is found frozen to the floor.
Not dead, mind you, not yet;
trapped on hands and knees —
four points stuck in ice.

Cold snapped her water pipes like kindling.
and the flood quickly chilled, lowering
to the point of freeze.
When she dropped awkwardly to her knees
to inspect the pipe, in that instant
liquid turned solid,
caught her in a pose
she held for two days
until someone thought to check.

•

At college, waking
to each bare branch and needle
encased in ice. The sun,
unable to break the cold, settled
for faceting the world in crystal.

Snow, unmarked even by birds,
mounded landscape into hummocks
of bicycle and bush. Paths and porches
anonymous, everything clean, glazed.

Out we'd come, moles in sunlight,
to listen to the strange music of trees
moving as if afraid to move, the ice
tinkling like chandeliers
set in motion by the movement of dancers.

Annie's Room

I wanted to sleep in the attic,
in the special room where Annie
once slept under the eaves;
Annie long-gone into war factories
south of the tracks.

My mother said no,
because of fire, she said,
so I practiced crawling out
the small window
onto the slanted roof, calculated
the leap to the chestnut tree.

I wanted to be near my father.
He was stored in boxes
in the tower room: his books,
sermons, black robe, his clarinet
with silver bands, silver keys

and in a corner, the gilded bust
my mother made: surreal,
the mask of a missing man,
missing arms, shoulders,
missing heart.

Other People's Pictures

Two little girls in fluffy white dresses,
sleeves puffed into wings.
Sisters.
A word I cherish.

An uncomfortable baby
held askew by her big brother
wishing the picture-taking over.

Another child sits on her grandfather's knee;
family groups of four or more.
I have none of these.

No father, grandfather, no brother
to tease. No sister-ally
though we were a family of women.

No rough beards, no watch pockets
to hide a secret coin, no deep chuckle
that might have taken my side.

No one to teach me the finer points
of trees, no one to confide in,
argue with, tattle on.

Another picture:
small girl sits hunched on the back steps,
toes pointing together, face sad.

Although her hair is dark,
the steps different, another house,
I know that child

and the long afternoon shadows that crawl
across the grass and up the stairs,
the falling sun in her eyes.

Hidden Up

In the center of the yard,
like a gift from Jack and his six beans,
is a chestnut worthy of the village smithy.

Its vast trunk crowns well above
the third story and the roof.
Each spring it unfurls mittens of downy celadon

that turn into green spaniel ears,
and white spikes of flowers
shoot up like fountains.

Once I learn to get up that tree;
once I creep and climb
behind the shadow of leaves,

even my movements are hidden.
From the kitchen window I hear
voices murmur; from the porch

the creak of wicker,
squeak of the green glider
as legs swing them in adult rhythms.

In my tree I am sailing the South Pacific,
fighting enemies in jungles and small villages,
capturing spies and bandits

as the sun takes its slow and ponderous course
dappling through branches until it reaches
the break in the leaves that means supper.

Windfall

The apple, not perfect,
but not yet visited by ant or beetle,
lay on its side in the timothy,
hard to see but for its last splash of red.

You picked it up, offered it on open palm
and I took it — despite what seemed to be
bird damage to one side, took it and
rubbed it on my sleeve, polishing its sphere
until it seemed to beckon.

I smiled at you, raised the apple
to my teeth
and bit it to its core.

It had not been long on the ground,
still juiced, still plumped and crunchy.
It could have been a Connecticut MacIntosh
so strong was the awakened memory
of being young and working my Aunt Claire's
fruit stand on the county road.

All those apples then, when orchards
were full of diversity. Customers
with favorites — baskets, bushels
the lugs of tumbled globes.
College-bound, we'd load the back seat
with apples, enough to make the transition
from summer toward winter.

I looked at your dear face,
late afternoon sun on your cheek,
turned the apple to its best side
and held it out.

Making the Cut

Born perfect,
tiny fingers with those sweet pearl nails,
eyes open, unblinking, full
of all they brought with them and have yet
to forget.

And we let the surgeon cut their bodies,
their most tender members,
They don't feel pain, they cry
only from surprise.

What were we thinking?
To take a piece of muscle and nerve,
slice it,
turn it back on itself.
Some improvement of cleanliness?
Some sacrifice to a male god?
Some impertinence that we
could improve on God's design?

My son has a son
fresh from the womb.
Perfect, he tells me at 4 a.m.,
perfect.

at your own risk

Along the Path

On the flanks of Mt. Tam, a path
opens, not seen before.
I veer left out of noon sun
into filtered light.

Warming ground pushes rein orchids
up with their colonnades of white trumpets;
wild iris wait below.
Air stirs with the oil of eucalyptus,

scent of my grandmother's aches.
Noises begin to whisper through the air,
first a chatter of bird feet along bark,
then the tiptoe step of two mule deer

who stop when I look: Simon Says.
Where the path leads does not concern me.
It is spring, Earth has opened her body
for swelling seeds and thrusts of stem.

I think back to a childhood path
when I feared copperheads on any sunlicked rock.
My eyes snap side to side
from ridge to low river stone, so I don't see
the man until he looms before me,
his organ rising
red from his open trousers.
My heart beating Retreat,
I say *Good Morning* and pass him by.

Now the Tam path seems a little darker.
Though the snakes are different
their heads are still wedge-shaped, their rocks
sun-warmed, their dry skin camouflaged.

Along this path will come other hikers
but not today. The deer are paused,
their eyes fixed on me, their ears big
as conchs. We stand, all of us, ears open

to the breaking leaves, ready
to flash white and flee.

That Red Girl

She wasn't really picking flowers, you know,
that red girl — she was stalling.
Another Monday visit to the old lady
who looked like her mother shriveled,
a mean old lady made of pinches
with a tongue like a bone stripped bare
and sticking out of the skin.

While Red teased the petals off the foxgloves,
her grandmother was likely laying traps
for gophers, dusting flowers with
snail poison, beer for the wasps, soapy water
for the beetles she didn't like, and plotting
how to get that leering wolf —

wolf that fancied her nightgown and bedcap —
cross-dressing wolf, trans-species wolf,
always wanting to get into her knickers —
relishing the lace, the elastic tight on his waist,
the way his foolish great wand of a tail
stuck out the back.

Grandmother, handy with a hammer, built
impregnable bureaus for her corsets, lacy slips,
iron-barred the closets so the ball gowns
were tantalizingly out of reach, leaving a place
for the wolf-stole she was planning —
though that mangy pelt was past its prime.

This game they'd been playing for years —
the wolf trotting along the path after puffing at piglets
and slobbering over sheep, and that stupid boy
who kept calling his name, *Wolf, Wolf,*
until the only person who came when he called
was the creature he called,

and then on to Grandmother's — slipping past
the red girl dragging her shoes in the leaves,
her steps slower and slower. Yes,
on to the grandmother, warty old adversary,
his sinewy old Doppelgänger, his nasty old stew.

Red Flash

A fox hangs out near the back barn,
occasional red flash that you only think
you've seen because it can't be verified,
he's that quick. He's never
near the mid-barn though sometimes grass
is bent in a hollow that might fit his shape, and
certainly not the near-barn though the chicken
population fluctuates in an odd way. Still,
there's no way in, no holes dug
around the deep, stiff fence, no red fur
caught like sunset on barbed wire.

Boards of the hen house are freshly painted
and show no scrape of claw, no scrawl of teeth
and yet the hens go, without a single strangled squawk,
disappear when the moon is down and shadows
blend into dark.

The fox has marked his territory on our minds,
We sleep uneasy, don't trust the tongue and grooved walls,
the fence firm and gridded in 4 inch rectangles.
How does he slip through our dreams and into the
anxious roost of hens. What is the rooster doing
while his girls are harvested? Does he blackmail
his harem into affection, *My Dears, I know a fox.*
The choice should not be hard . . .

Rapunzel's Mirror

My dear, he's not worth it, what man, what real man, would climb a woman's hair to get at her. Yes, I know, you encourage him, but it will be to your sorrow. Hair is only hair after all, and every woman has some. Let him climb your hair and he'll be climbing hair at every window. Besides, it's not good for your tresses, my pet, my foolish reflection. When you stand before me and gaze in our eyes, I cannot see all your hair, but I know it flows down your back to your feet, curls around your legs like a boa wrapping its prey. Dear one, cut it off now, before your foolish heart throws you out the window after it. It has happened to others. You are more than golden hair, but he may never know more than the flutter of his climb — the hand over hand shinny up a river of hair, while you grit your teeth with the weight of him and your scalp stretches to the point of breaking. I know you have locked your mother out, as she has locked you in. She will pound at the door, at the extra feet tapping her ceiling. She will shake the doorknob at any whisper of conversation. She knows you do not talk to yourself. She will shout and scream and call for your father, who, if he hears, will shoulder his bow and come from the hunt to the hunt. She will step out the door, see the torn ivy, the scratched sill, and wisps of your foolish hair sliding back up the wall — and you — hair intact but little else, must use these moments to make of him a future, for there is little time before he wakes to morning and decides to climb down, seek out the next hirsute maiden — or stay with you and risk all for your golden hair.

Purple and Gold

Episcopal Purple said the Bishop his smile benign and uneven as he lifted the cluster of grapes not yet pressed into wine not yet transmogrified into real blood blue blood we all tested it as children were as royal as we were convinced we were our blood flowed a river down our wrists inner sides of elbows Johnny Chickory and I pricked our fingers and pressed them blood to blood brothers in truth and trust a genderless thing until he turned eleven and was too embarrassed to be caught playing catch with a _ _ _ _ or was it that I was a better athlete better than most of the scrawny freckled boys and they knew it even though my mother admonished like a metronome that boring cadence *let the boys win* because she believed I'd never get a husband all men would be poisoned by my peccadilloes of muscle and brain I thought boys were a little dull and flatulent to boot those good at games usually had to be tutored but of course I wasn't supposed to show I was smart either what a posse of persona we were all the little girls accepting absurd requirements and of course we couldn't wear purple either that was for girls at First Baptist who went around like ribbon candy in chaotic combinations of colors forbidden to us or the girls at St. Mary's by the Sea who wore pierced earrings that glinted in the sun real gold a king's ransom oh we'd read Treasure Island and we wanted those tiny forbidden globes

Leather Boys

They lived in town, in houses that touched,
houses that needed paint, and money for the rent.
We never talked of their parents.
We didn't know their families,
what they did on Sundays.

They were the boys our mothers feared,
alien boys, and we the moths drawn to their light.

They were the boys who crossed themselves
before games, kissed the plated medals
around their necks. Boys who cursed
with horned fingers, or a fist
jammed in the crotch of an elbow.

They wore their hair in ducks' asses and smoked.
Their fingers were yellow at the tips
and their breath — their yellow breath.
They had cars, not the Plymouths
of our fathers, but well-tuned jalopies
that they assembled at Elder's garage.
Turquoise or lime, with cracked seats
and a neckers' knob so you could ride close,
his left hand on the knob and his right hand
across your shoulder, sneaking forays
down toward your breast.

They were the older boys,
their bristles glistened in the afternoon light.
Our mothers rolled their eyes, kept those boys
off the party lists.

But they were there,
at all the parties — outside — in the katydid nights —
the flicker of cigarettes glowing — the rasp of a match —
the soft creak of leather jackets — their voices low.
We felt them out there.
We welcomed them out there,
the occasional bark of a laugh, quick, then gone.

Close Encounter

This smart ass's been following me, waving
and calling out his window, *pull over girly*, and
I know you'd like me, and riding my tail
'til I'm a nervous mess. So I see this cement truck,
you know, the peppermint striped belly
going around to keep the stuff
mixing and I pull along side and it's driven by
Burt Reynolds, well not Burt himself, you know
but near enough and no need for a rug neither.
I tell him this guy behind me is *harassing* me and
I can't shake him and the guy pulls his
come 'ere-machine right in close behind the truck,
engine humming, his tongue running across
his upper lip, and ol' Burt
gives me a wink and lays a dump
right on the guy's hood and up the windshield
and takes off and the guy jumps out and I
follow the truck close so the jerk can't get
the license and he's screaming like his nuts
was in a wringer and I'm laughin' and the truck
pulls off like a fat elephant, me following
and Burt waves his big ol' hand
out the window as we round the corner
and I blow him a kiss.

The Body Wants to Be Useful

The body, supplying us with levers and pulleys,
wants to be used, kept in good order,
drops of oil dripped into joints. The body,
having no thoughts or emotions of its own,
is highly attuned to the other systems of our being,
and sometimes against its better nature,
but hangs back now, lazy and reluctant.

The body has instincts,
knows it is happier when tuned like a engine.
The body wants to be a Ferrari
but has settled into being an old pickup
that needs a lot of work or it will end up
with grasses growing through the floorboards.

I talk to my body, whine, apologize for betrayals,
and pretending it isn't there.
It pays me back by becoming the Tin Woodsman.
Sometimes I cannot face the body;
step out of it — move to one side
and pretend it isn't there. This is unfair, I know
because the body is only trying to please,
it's getting mixed messages — desire and ennui —
it doesn't know which master to obey —
it's own inner, quiet, voice
or the parliament of outside voices of temptation.
It lacks the will power to consider
what's right for the body, what it needs to be useful.

I bring it oil, and balms of sweet smelling lotions —
I beg it to do what's right,
not follow the example I've set for it —
not listen to the easy chorusing
of the indolent, oh yes, the hedonist.

At Your Own Risk

Waves break hard on a line of rocks,
wash over their table-surfaces like anger.
No one here bothers with suits, we like our bodies
bare and bold. Seaweed catches
on outcrops like green mementos.

When the ninth wave comes, it towers
before the crest collapses and hits shore
with a thud that shakes our striped towels.
I look up from my book and wonder
if the captain's leg is wood or the whale white.

Along the shore a rip tide pulls its turmoil
out to sea and one thin lady with it.
To her children she's irreplaceable, to the sea
she's but another piece of flotsam.

A Boat of Glass

I.

No delicate craft but blocky,
stacks of smoked quartz — an azure cube
wherein no captain takes the helm.
Yet, despite its girth and grand solidity,
it seems to float and I imagine
it gracing the horizon like a translucent log of light
before it drips over the edge of the world
vanishing.

II.

Now they conjecture, surmise, decree
that the universe is flat, O hail, Columbus —
that shooting two beams of parallel light
out across the gardens of space — and they tell us
they will never merge in the distance, but instead
remain apart into the forever darkness.
The universe stretches out its fingers —
no graceful curves — no horizon — ever.

III.

Omatund, you sly devil,
I never see you anymore, not even
a glimpse of your back hurrying away.
Fill me in on life. Is there no beginning —
no answer or end? We simply
walk along Water Street forever,
keeping our even pace, our arms-length
distance — our parallel paths.

IV.

Like ships, Omatund and I,
silent as streaks of light, walking
the harbor street in some peaceful
state of non-expectation. I have not
seen him in seven years, seven seas,
seven tidal voids. Now he says
nothing, walks step by even step
beside me, his arms swinging, the solid
block of his body keeping pace with mine.
The smoky quartz of his hair,
his azure eyes — smokestack of a man,
my companion in silence.

V.

We come to harbor
at the lamplight on the corner, where he turns,
wraps me in his arms
and falls off the edge of the world.

Time Off

A brindled dog lifts its leg
as day surges toward dark, pulling us after.
I look for you in corners of my unblinking eye
but there's no refuge here.
No man is as good as a laugh,
I tell myself these things — even meaning some of them.
What I want is time off the trail
where wildflowers are not yet covered with dust.
As a single deer, withers rippling, cocks its mule-ears,
this is a good place to taste the seeds of Earth.
I pull my collar tight around my neck
wishing for the lick of sunrays.
The land stretches its long thighs to couple with the sea.
Salt is in the air, delicious on my lips.

hold and release

It Happens with Children, Often,
Those Things That Scare Us

1.

Sometimes it comes in dreams — night
after sphincter night — the children

up in a tree — small, three on a horizontal branch
that should hold them, but they begin to slip —
like eels over a weir, they slip
with their smooth skins and their open faces.

Glide easily off the branch and unafraid
start to fall — my trio of the future —
falling like snow from that great height —
and I — I am below, my arms moving

right to center to left — back and forth —
which one — which?

They fall — none faster than the others
but moving apart nonetheless —
widening the gap between them.
I must now follow my arms —
must rush left, stumble right.

They fall — silent as breathing — faces showing now,
hair floating around them —
their eyes look down — fastened on mine.
And I know — I know

2.

We take them to Yosemite, bigger now
but not very. Climb the wet, slick, trail
past Vernal to Nevada Falls, and the blond one,
the smallest — still chunky but beginning to learn risk —
beginning to sense defiance — leans through the rails
over the torrent. I hiss at her
and she comes back, reluctant, sullen.

Next time I look, my heart
thuds like fresh-caught fish beginning to sense
that air is death — for this child
with her red spot of sweater
has climbed outside the rails —

rails keeping her not from the falls
but from me — rails slick from many hands —
too fat for her small hands — and the branch
of the tree-dream clicks into place.

And I say — from my distance — *come back
please*, pretending to look away, pretending
I am not edging my feet forward, my arms
struggling not to lash out and grab,
pretending I do not see
that wall of water that roars for her.

Early Morning, Yosemite

Like an old matron on her way to market,
the bear came lumbering around the corner
of the cabin, placing her plantigrade paws
clomp clomp, first the right legs, then the left,
rumbling as if with lumbago, as if with old stiff knees,

not sniffing the air, not hungry it seemed,
only about her business, and the sun
glistened through her fur as it prickled her back
and all of us stopped dead in our tracks as if
Simon Says said *STOP* and we did.

And across the meadow I saw my small daughter —
her red sweater like a toreador's cape —
sitting on a log with her friend, Julie,
their blond heads close together,
gossiping their four-year-old gossip —
like neighbors over a cup of coffee at the back fence —

and neither noticing the bear approaching,
and me watching uncertain how to handle this
and Julie's mother gripping my arm with her long nails
and the bear walking her slow market lurch
and the girls talking
and the sun blasting the trees
throwing shadows like tall men across the grass
and the bear
only the bear
moving.

The Swallow

My daughter is a swallow
who does not, any season,
return

she swooped out,
stroking hard
her arrowed wings

with no intention then
or now
of turning back

Another Birthday

No one asked you to leave,
but your road led out, and out,

only one lane, going one way.
Daughter, I'm losing track of you.

I don't remember a time
you weren't angry, leaning away.

All the damaged years,
a life-time of birthdays on calendars

showing pictures of other places
with perfect landscapes.

First Responder

I. Deep Green Chute

There's the beep
and the crackle of the pager
as he listens to its call for help —
a boy, thirteen, swallowed by the river.

He's the closest,
the first responder.
A mother chalky and shaking
grabs his arms with her nails,

Find him, find my boy,
her voice a constantly re-opening sore.
Why are you standing here?

Ma'am, this is not a river to enter easy,
not alone, even knowing it as I do,
especially knowing it as I do.

Her face turns red,
bone-white, again red,
like an autumn leaf faceting in the wind.

Her eyes search his for hope.
His face says hope
is always possible, but unlikely.

He knows there are many ways to lose your life.
This may be the easiest — to step into a river
still bulked by spring thaw.

He sees where the river humps over rocks,
where the deep green chute pulls down and left,
sees the water comes out slow and straight

through a strainer hole — that's where they'll find him,
the boy who thought he knew more
than a river.

II. Fencing the River

The banks swarm with men, radios crackle.
The boy's father has returned ashen.
He's waited too long, spent too much time

racing along the river
calling, praying it's a prank,
for that miracle he knows won't come.

Now all he can hope for is a body.
Something to hold wet in his arms
and croon to it his love and sorrow.

The river keeps pouring its mastery
down the course, pressure, like a hand,
holds a boy head first in its embrace.

More Search and Rescue bring a pick-up
with two by fours. Fighting their way
against the current, men force the boards
one by one into a fence upriver from the rocks.

Slowly it rises, the water parts and rages
around its ends, while below the fence,
the river ebbs, one, two, three feet.

The fence builders throw their bodies against
the wood, against the force of the river behind it.
Now the First Responder and two others dive

and dive again, and again, and finally drag the boy
back out the rock-funnel and up to the surface.
They bring him to shore, to his mother, his father.

III. Next Day

The First Responder walks to breakfast.
Sunlight slants through trees,
scallops off the river's rapids.
The boy's mother stands on the shore
staring into its restored power.
He goes and stands next to her,
and again, gently this time,
she puts her hands on his arms.

My Son's Hands

His hands are like mine,
stubby, "farmer's hands" we call them,
fingers short and close to the palm,
but they are *not* my hands,
my blood does not flow through them

and his are hard used — the knuckles
overlarge, the skin scraped and toughened
from contact with the rock.

Here are the marks of clefts
where he's jammed his fist into a crack
and holds himself on the mountain
by the strength of his arm, his wrist.

Here the callused fingertips
that grip tiny ledges above his head
in the language of the blind.

I think of him on high domes and spires
I think of his hands
and how I depend on them
to bring him down again.

I remember x-rays of his boy-fingers,
the ivoried growth rings
of rheumatoidal joints. He shows me,
still, how he cannot close his hands
completely — the ivory still there
that should have been absorbed

and these incomplete hands
hold him in air
as currents of wind hold the bird.

Even now, the Himalayas
are both rising and eroding.

He can be a scratchy guy,
but on the rock he is a poem,
the lines of his climbing
full of cadence and rhythm.

He says the mountain is a spirit king
and he feels its face with his hands.
This knowledge works into his fingers
and informs his life.

Rock seems permanent to me
and he seems always young
but time has its way with both.

The rock fractures and breaks.
Sun, even the wind, moves
across its face — scours and claims it,
piece by silent piece.

Unfamiliar Foliage

My mother will not move to California:
unfamiliar foliage,
salt from a different ocean,

and I can't easily reach her
now that she is willing to be reached
now that she has come out the dark side of January
and taken on new skin.

I used to go east
not toward the rising sun,
but an uncomfortable setting.
I took flights back into my past
where she waited honed for attack.

My mother, having reached the age
of speaking out, did so,
sharp as a knife with the new penny
still taped to the shank.

She nicked at me
like the boy in my son's class
who cut himself,
shallow slices on arms and thighs.

My mother watched
the minutes track down faster each day
and reckoning her job unfinished,
went after me like a whittler with a deadline
who would be faulted for my incompletion.

But lately, having met the pale stranger,
taken in his gaunt limbs, his shadowed eyes,
something dropped from her,
like skin peeling off a burn.

She has adjusted to death,
put her feet up on the long slope
and no longer sees me in inches and details.
This makes things easier
and harder.

Deep in the Roots

My mother is old and frail.
Soon she will fade like the leaves
and fall into drift
and the prints of her story
will remain unrecognized.

Last time I visited,
we recited in unison
James James Morrison Morrison.
Word perfect
she plucked it from memory.

It's not too late to solicit stories,
the colors and details of her entire stretch of century
and yet it seems like badgering now,
insisting on "presence"
before her head begins to nod,
the fingers relax their grip
and let papers flutter to the floor.

I listened to a ranger far in the north
talk about the conversation of trees,
how scientists have measured their warnings
and commiserations,
an electric code.

At the whack of the ax, trees
reach out toward each other
along a network of roots
like my mother and me — for so long
the two of us alone facing out into the world
and still we whisper along our root hairs
small messages heard deeply by the other.

One day she starts to tell me
where to find her records: lawyer,
broker, phone numbers.
I know what she is saying.

The Box

The box sits before me
cardboard with a slip-in lid.
Inside is a black box
on which I cannot get purchase,
cannot remove the one from the other.

I turn the first box on end
and the black box slides out
like a birthing baby.
I break the seal with my fingernail;
it feels like sacrilege.

Inside is the plastic bag
of bone-grit
hunched and unruly.
There is no sound as the contents shift.
I study its grayness,
the quality of its grain.
It is not more than I expected
or heavier — it just is.

I lift it out
and cup my hands around it.
I am a potter,
know the feel of basic clay.
I hold it lovingly, wrapping
my warm fingers around its cold weight.
I smell its slightly charred,
charnel, earthy smell.
Carefully, I open
the neck of the bag,
wet my finger and taste
the contents, sandlike on my tongue,
close up the bag and lower my face
pressing it against her ashes.

Hold and Release

My mother's bones —
now powder-fine and gritty,
sink into the waves like mica,
like the minnows

I used to chum for, when we
stood on this very dock
and fished for shiners pulled
from this salty, terrific water.

I am scattering my mother
into the seasons, into the eternals
that make up our lives:
fire, earth, air, wood and now water —

The smell of brine is heavy;
tides pulled back deeply from shore;
a slight breeze, enough
to carry her from my open hands.

It is a finish and a beginning, release and retain
in one, two, three casts of the hands,
moisture in the air turning my flesh grey
with the clay of my mother.

Here where we dove and stroked,
sailed and laughed, I return her
to those early days when a war was over
and our hearts were ever lifted by summer.

night of mirrors

Considering Endless Night

As a child, after I'd turned off the flashlight,
I'd try to imagine what endless night would be,
that after the certain number of hours,
no dome of sun would break open the horizon,
no long strobes of light would search
for trees and rooftops. I knew little then
about creatures who prefer night,
those of deep sea trenches who depend on dark.

At the aquarium,
I stand in a room round with jellyfish,
drifting in starclouds of plankton,
silently pulsing in unaccustomed light.
It doesn't help them avoid each other, rather
they glide through their liquid world,
bumping, nudging, caught and carrying,
as if blind, as if whatever they touched
was *there* — nothing more.

The gauzy openwork parachutes
they use to make the world's longest migration
and do it nightly, rising
2000 feet to feed at the surface,
falling before dawn to their mid-sea existence.
Never to see the light, or each other's waltzing,
their long, lovely trains drifting behind
like Belgian lace.

What is written on the boneless jellyfish,
what lovely inscriptions does each one
read from the other
in their minuets of mating, their waltz
through lifetimes in the dark?

Looking Toward Waves

A raven hunches like a nun over a breviary.

A pod of black seals off the point
turns into surfers that rise, graceful
on the tide and glide to shore.

Pelicans cross west like bombers,
their stealth beaks turned
toward the wave that's coming,

and down the beach
with no destination in mind
a brown dog races ahead of his ears

In the sand, a child has built Stonehenge
around a courtyard of serpentine pebbles —

small fortress that the sea will claim
as easily as jungle swallows
the jade altars of the Olmecs.

I stand in this place that always works for me,
the thunder of surf, the scree of gullcalls,

as the ocean plays the shore,
again and again calls my name.

On the Movement of Petals and Feathers

Brisk wind whips the tamaracks
     and the white hollyhocks kneel
          before it like nuns,

like egrets blowing on the marsh
     their long angles firm in the bottom,
          eyes cocked, never wavering.

Wind takes its share of petals
     from the hollyhock, scatters them
          in a shower of soft snow

and one white feather graces the air
     like a sign, a moment of morning peace
          as if time stopped and only the feather

          continued to breathe.

Time Runs Past but Never Out of Sight

I didn't have time to stop last night
as the moon lipped over the ridge,
threw down its citron skirts across the Bay.
                              I should have
pulled over and drawn in the night
as a boon against hours of toil.
                              Driving home today,
I was startled to see pelicans on a drift of wood
bodies aligned, heads turned toward the line of cars
like stags at a cotillion,
                              I knew
I should park and drink them in, poised,
their shadows on the water, but the clock
is king, the shoulders of tarmac narrow.
                              Are the pelicans
still there? Time has moved me forward
to a spot beyond their reach.
                              It's the same with children,
how they linger in certain scenes, frozen
in their short pants, their limber gaits,
                              and now
their children stand beside them, same size,
same carefully shaped heads and arms;
                              time has been routed,
biding, until conjured again —
those strobes of certainties about who
was fair, who dark, or thin.
                              Now that time has run out
for my mother, she can be any age I choose —
hair dark as ebony, spine ramrod straight —
                              she can ride
in the black Chevy or the green one, balance
on the Schwinn she rode around town,
so interested in front yard scenes —
                              once again
she'll forget to pedal, fall over
like a Keystone Kop — the spied-upon neighbors
running down the block to resurrect her.
                              These snippets of time suspended
                              *

come in unannounced, remind me
that when I think I don't have time,
                              there are moments
more important than calendars and watches:
to pull the day to a halt
for a white sail against the open ocean,
a small boy hunkered down by a slow-tracing snail,
or a girl with a straw hat,
one of the long blue ribbons caught in her teeth.

Sunstones

for Dick O'Hanlon

Set the vertical stone, then the meridian stone:
create an equinoctial passage between them
heading west toward setting sun and the door of death,
while moonset and sunrise align in the vestibules of time.

The geography of the heavens,
the horizons of Earth,
great primed verticals of buildings and trees reaching —
our own place in the curve of landscape.

Though we hold a position on Earth
and in the solar system, most of us
have lost our bridges to the stars,
the geometry of the constellations.

We're a narrow plane around the sun
allowing eclipse in the vast moonful sky.
Trace along the great bear to Earth's axis,
faint and unchanging; night or day: we revolve.

Consider local solar noon, how it differs from your watch,
seeking its own shadow-loss, its own solstic-equinal arc.
It moves, muttered Galileo, defying the cardinals,
and we move, a cycle within a revolution within an orbit.

Beyond the Bear's Paw

Hold a single grain of sand,
only one, against the night sky,
there, where it's darkest, where
the familiar bear rumbles, apparently alone.

Imagine that behind that speck of quartz
a distant telescope has recorded
an infinity of galaxies pocking the void.

The mind fills with improbabilities.
And yet, there they are: galaxies
spinning in graceful spirals,
their lazy arms curved in the solar winds.

Sooner Comes the Dusk

Last night I turned back the clocks,
convinced myself of an extra hour,
read in bed until my elbows hurt,
but my body wasn't fooled.
It woke early this morning convinced
it knew the time.

Darkness falls faster each day —
great stones of night signal
the harvest is ending, the lengthening sleep
of winter closing in.

The sun is heating other shores.
People hanging upside down
on the bottom of Earth
are putting away their sweaters
and searching for swimsuits and lotion.

Here we are hauling out sweaters, checking
to see if mothballs have kept their promise.
My husband puts the hard top on his convertible,
and the dog, going by the light
thinks it is time to eat, when it isn't.

What does he know of clocks — or care.
He tells time by the sun, by the light
that hits the kitchen floor at a certain angle.
He is confused today, when I leave,
because I do not feed him, and he knows
it is time.

I watch the Prussian blue slate of the bay
take on its winter lead, and the crab apple
is raining huge leaves, creating
a yellow circle beneath itself.

Around us the air thickens and grows chilled,
as all day the rocks whisper of night.

Winter Solstice

As fall moves 17 miles per day
    south heralding snow,
so the gray in my hair advances
    daily from the edges
across the crown and up from the nape.

In certain light, the hints
    of blond remain,
but comes a day as thick
    as the first real storms of solstice,
when the gray overtakes and settles.

Be quiet, heart, let the eyes
    feast slow and wet
upon the grizzled hand of time.
    The mark of wisdom seeping into bones.
What surrender in admission.

There is a ditch, wide
    and swampy that lies ahead
 Some dreaded haha that snags
    the wary, weary crone, slow
of step and tiring of effort.

But let this not be a time
    for despair to lower its heavy hand.
Oh, be still and think
    on all the supple years enjoyed
that may again, from time to time, hold sway.

Winter Light

It's coming, the night of mirrors,
creeping its long fingers of darkness
over roads and idled grasses.
It's when I grapple to hold
light in my hands, light
slipping free as water through my fist.

Lengthening night is a creature
I would keep at bay, but Earth
turns and the stars overhead cartwheel
into their new solstic positions.
Orion rises confident — hunter of midnight
and I know he stalks best in the dark
with his night-seeing eyes,
dog faithful at his heels.

Outside the raccoon stirs,
moon-eyes searching for corners
of water, the plodding skunk sharpens
his long nails on the backs of grubs
and the neighbor's cat moves in the bushes
clothed in shadow and insolence.

I put my pens away and step out
as the shawl of evening slips from the mountains.
Night has hold of my world,
paints Earth to its own sweet harvest,
dares us to slow and rest,
then invites us to the table of edges.

Missing Stars

To leave behind our stars —
          to so occlude
                    their high wonders
that but a few are granted in the night.

We, an ever-invading cog
          in the spaces of earth,
                    have lighted the stars from the sky.
We have, seemingly, tamed them.

          Those stunning,
                    those alien stones.

And yet, an open ocean
          with but a spar,
                    a sail, and running lights —
and the stars take back their glory.

          Those touchstones of fire
                    burning open the cloth of night.

They spill across the sky more
          numerous than sands.
                    They carpet the darkness,
our wildflowers of midnight.

Star Catching

I am the one who goes out to catch stars
    floating my long arms beyond the sky
    pluck them — one by tinselly one
I am the one packing stars in my pockets
    removing their rust each morning
    with a paisley shawl
I am the one who hangs stars from my bed ceiling
    lets them swing in a tableau of glitter
I am the one who mothers them
    like fledglings kept captive
    in a snowhouse of candles
I am the one who refuses morning
    who pulls back the curtains of age
    thumps tomorrow on its entering nose
I am the one who stirs clouds
    with a plum branch and reaches
    through for the stars that hide
I am the one who maps the cosmos anew —
    aligning constellations to my own designs
I am the one who sighs and sets them to motion
    and as a dancer awakens a chandelier
    I move then to their diminishing corrections
I am the one who packs midnight in a valise
    of glove leather
    and hauls it home full of stars
If you want them you must come to me,
    I will match star to sapphire
    and let you float one home on a string
I am the one who knows the stories of stars
    whispered, a chaos of eddas
    frosting my lobes with their hoary voices
        For as I've told you
I am the one who loves stars
    through a wilderness of branches
    where they wink and titter
and I am the one who climbs the tattered trees
    to pluck stars loose of their anchors
    and throw one over the side
    as a kedge to pull me home.

Stones of Memory

The stones of memory are of different geologies.
Some are river rocks torn loose
by the current of a full flood,
tumbled over and around until all that's left
is a generic tale of time passing
and rhythms reduced.
                Some are slippers of chert
on which you get no footing,
and which skip out of the mind
like a ferret, sneaky and apt to disappear
just when you think to grasp it:
                the chert, the weasel, the memory
bounding, leaping down hillsides
ever out of reach — leaving
hints, occasional glimpses and then gone.
                Or pegmatite, sharp edged —
no end of pounding can soften its granite jags.
Unlikely to move or reveal its underside,
these rocks are full of what you will tell
grandchildren,
                small beings that know
before you do, that you are old as hills,
and give the same weight and distance
as the mountains that loom behind their house —
                What can I tell
of how it was, or will be for them.
They won't believe. I didn't.
                Yet, cranking ice cream
to get that sweet taste of summer on the tongue;
a cart pulled by a horse, the only way to get
from the aunts' — to the cabins on the lake.
What will they tell?
                One asks if his father
could do a 360 on his skateboard, a 720, a 900,
something *his* heroes do every day.
                What kind of geode
holds the memories of his father.
I am interested in their geology,
their mother lode two generations removed,
*

topo-map to their drives and fears.
                    What kind of ghosts will they see?
Who whispers in their ears,
and what kind of pebbles will tumble
                    in the speech of their curiosities?

Biographical Note

CB Follett is the winner of the 2001 National Poetry Book Award from Salmon Run Press. She has had poems published in *Calyx*, *Green Fuse*, *Peregrine*, *The Cumberland Review*, *Rain City Review*, *Ambit*, *The MacGuffin*, *Birmingham Poetry Review*, *Black Bear Review*, *New Letters Review*, *Psychological Perspectives*, *Without Halos*, *The Iowa Woman*, *Heaven Bone*, *Americas Review*, and *The Taos Review*, among others. Her work has appeared in many anthologies and has received honors in competitions, among them the Billee Murray Denny Poetry Award, the *New Letters* Prize, the Ann Stanford Prize, the Glimmer Train Poetry Contest, and several contests of the Poetry Society of America. Five of her poems have been nominated for a Pushcart Prize.

Hold and Release is Follett's fifth published collection of poetry. She is editor and publisher of Arctos Press and coeditor and publisher of *RUNES, A Review of Poetry*.

Follett is also an artist, with artwork in many private collections around the world.

Other poetry and short fictions available from Time Being Books

Yakov Azriel
Threads from a Coat of Many Colors: Poems on Genesis

Edward Boccia
No Matter How Good the Light Is: Poems by a Painter

Louis Daniel Brodsky
The Capital Café: Poems of Redneck, U.S.A.

Catchin' the Drift o' the Draft *(short fictions)*

Combing Florida's Shores: Poems of Two Lifetimes

The Complete Poems of Louis Daniel Brodsky: Volumes One–Three

Disappearing in Mississippi Latitudes: Volume Two of *A Mississippi Trilogy*

The Eleventh Lost Tribe: Poems of the Holocaust

Falling from Heaven: Holocaust Poems of a Jew and a Gentile *(Brodsky and Heyen)*

Forever, for Now: Poems for a Later Love

Four and Twenty Blackbirds Soaring

Gestapo Crows: Holocaust Poems

A Gleam in the Eye: Poems for a First Baby

Leaky Tubs *(short fictions)*

Mississippi Vistas: Volume One of *A Mississippi Trilogy*

Mistress Mississippi: Volume Three of *A Mississippi Trilogy*

Nuts to You! *(short fictions)*

Paper-Whites for Lady Jane: Poems of a Midlife Love Affair

Peddler on the Road: Days in the Life of Willy Sypher

Pigskinizations *(short fictions)*

Rated Xmas *(short fictions)*

Shadow War: A Poetic Chronicle of September 11 and Beyond, Volumes One–Five

Showdown with a Cactus: Poems Chronicling the Prickly Struggle Between the Forces of Dubya-ness and Enlightenment, 2003–2006

This Here's a Merica *(short fictions)*

The Thorough Earth

Three Early Books of Poems by Louis Daniel Brodsky, 1967–1969: *The Easy Philosopher, "A Hard Coming of It" and Other Poems,* and *The Foul Rag-and-Bone Shop*

Toward the Torah, Soaring: Poems of the Renascence of Faith

A Transcendental Almanac: Poems of Nature

Voice Within the Void: Poems of *Homo supinus*

Yellow Bricks *(short fictions)*

You Can't Go Back, Exactly

866-840-4334

http://www.timebeing.com

Harry James Cargas (editor)
Telling the Tale: A Tribute to Elie Wiesel on the Occasion of His 65th
  Birthday — Essays, Reflections, and Poems

Judith Chalmer
Out of History's Junk Jar: Poems of a Mixed Inheritance

Gerald Early
How the War in the Streets Is Won: Poems on the Quest of Love and Faith

Gary Fincke
Blood Ties: Working-Class Poems

Charles Adés Fishman
Chopin's Piano

Albert Goldbarth
A Lineage of Ragpickers, Songpluckers, Elegiasts & Jewelers: Selected
  Poems of Jewish Family Life, 1973–1995

Robert Hamblin
From the Ground Up: Poems of One Southerner's Passage to Adulthood

William Heyen
Erika: Poems of the Holocaust
Falling from Heaven: Holocaust Poems of a Jew and a Gentile *(Brodsky and Heyen)*
The Host: Selected Poems, 1965–1990
Pterodactyl Rose: Poems of Ecology
Ribbons: The Gulf War — A Poem

Ted Hirschfield
German Requiem: Poems of the War and the Atonement of a Third Reich Child

Virginia V. James Hlavsa
Waking October Leaves: Reanimations by a Small-Town Girl

866-840-4334

http://www.timebeing.com

Rodger Kamenetz
The Missing Jew: New and Selected Poems
Stuck: Poems Midlife

Norbert Krapf
Blue-Eyed Grass: Poems of Germany
Looking for God's Country
Somewhere in Southern Indiana: Poems of Midwestern Origins

Adrian C. Louis
Blood Thirsty Savages

Leo Luke Marcello
Nothing Grows in One Place Forever: Poems of a Sicilian American

Gardner McFall
The Pilot's Daughter

Joseph Meredith
Hunter's Moon: Poems from Boyhood to Manhood

Ben Milder
The Good Book Also Says . . . : Numerous Humorous Poems Inspired by
    the New Testament
The Good Book Says . . . : Light Verse to Illuminate the Old Testament
Love Is Funny, Love Is Sad
The Zoo You Never Gnu: A Mad Menagerie of Bizarre Beasts and Birds

Charles Muñoz
Fragments of a Myth: Modern Poems on Ancient Themes

Micheal O'Siadhail
The Gossamer Wall: Poems in Witness to the Holocaust

Joseph Stanton
A Field Guide to the Wildlife of Suburban O'ahu
Imaginary Museum: Poems on Art